MARK GRESCHNER

One Hundred Years of Heart

MARK GRESCHNER
One Hundred Years of Heart

Mark Greschner

Foreword by

Her Honour the Honourable Dr. Lynda M. Haverstock
Lieutenant Governor of Saskatchewan

ARTEC

Library and Archives Canada Cataloguing in Publication

Greschner, Mark
      Mark Greschner : one hundred years of heart / Mark Greschner ; foreword
by Lynda M. Haverstock ; [text, Marian J. Ready].

Includes index.
ISBN 0-9780529-0-0

      I. Centenarians--Saskatchewan--Portraits. 2. Saskatchewan--Biography.
I. Ready, Marian J. II. Title. III. Title: One hundred years of heart.

TR647.G74 2006   779'.2'097124   C2006-901624-0

Concept and photography by Mark Greschner
Book design by Brent Pylot
Text by Marian J. Ready

Printed and bound in Canada.

www.markgreschneronehundredyearsofheart.com

Artec Publishing
1350-A Rose Street
Regina, Sk   S4R 1Z8

To my beautiful wife, Cindy,
and my two wonderful children,
Drake and Orisha.
I love you.

Foreword

Age comes with many gifts: the satisfaction of accomplishment, the wisdom of experience, and the perspective of time.   One hundred year-old George Burns understood that the simple things in life are a gift. He said:

"Everyday happiness means getting up in the morning, and you can't wait to finish your breakfast. You can't wait to do your exercises. You can't wait to put on your clothes. You can't wait to get out – and you can't wait to come home, because the soup is hot."

This beautiful collection illustrates that, for many, age comes with the gift of laughter, as well. Each fascinating face is a canvas on which the adventures of a lifetime are painted.   These portraits speak to the intensely personal, but they also tell the story of a province. Those who were born into the new world of the twentieth century lived through extraordinary circumstances. They faced change and challenge with determination and enthusiasm. Our home is what it is today because of their boundless energy, unfailing optimism, and an abiding faith in a future even they could not imagine.

What better way to celebrate the centennial of our province than to honour those who built it. Mark Greschner's charming and powerful images are a magnificent tribute to 180 vibrant citizens who gave us the gift of Saskatchewan.

Dr. Lynda Haverstock
Lieutenant Governor
Province of Saskatchewan

ACKNOWLEDGEMENTS

Acknowledgements

Creating this book has been a labour of love. Throughout the project, I was surrounded by family and friends who believed in my vision. Their support encouraged me greatly and I thank them.

I thank the Saskatchewan Centennial Committee and the Saskatchewan Wheat Pool for their generous contributions. From the beginning, they understood the importance of creating a lasting record of the people who helped build our province.

Two talented individuals provided their invaluable assistance on the project. I thank Brent Pylot for his outstanding design of the book and for carefully attending to the prepress and the detailed work of preparing the portrait files for printing. Marian J. Ready used her remarkable writing ability to blend my collection of notes and biographical materials into thoughtful expressions of the lives of the centenarians.

I am especially grateful to the centenarians for sharing their time and memories. Their images are captured by the camera, but their spirit is boundless.

January 25, 2006

Proud to celebrate 100 years of heart in Saskatchewan.

Throughout 2005 we paid tribute to the heart and spirit of Saskatchewan people.

Saskatchewan Centennial 2005 is proud to be a partner in the production of the book, *Mark Greschner One Hundred Years of Heart*, in the province's centennial year.

Saskatchewan's centennial provides us with the opportunity to celebrate, honour and thank our province's centenarians. Throughout 2005, to pay tribute to this group of incredible people who have given so much to our province, Saskatchewan Centennial 2005 recognized 359 centenarians with special honours including a commemorative medallion and certificate. These are people who shaped our great province, who have homesteaded and farmed our land, worked in our industries, built our cities, taught us and our children and defended our freedom.

We are thankful to Saskatchewan's centenarians for sharing their memories, traditions, experiences and talents, and for continuing to make significant contributions to their families and communities. They possess wisdom and insight. The photographs and narratives in this amazing book honour their stories well.

Like so many others, I am proud to celebrate the individuals who have set examples of resilience, ingenuity, sustained courage and "100 Years of Heart."

Happy centennial, Saskatchewan!

Glenn Hagel, MLA
Chair of Saskatchewan Centennial 2005

We love this place. Saskatchewan! www.sask2005.ca

February 13, 2006

To understand Saskatchewan, you have to understand its heart.

Our province has a spirit that runs through it unlike any place else; a spirit that reflects the hopes, dreams and determination of the pioneers who laid the foundation for what we enjoy today.

For over 100 years, we have benefited from their tireless efforts. More than that, we have collectively taken on the best traits of a remarkable generation that set a high standard for achievement and stood fearless in the face of challenges. They were inventors and innovators; people willing to find solutions and embrace change.

These are the people who built our province – and built Saskatchewan Wheat Pool. Today, we follow in their footsteps as individuals, as a business and as a province that remains unique within the landscape of Canada.

Their stories are our story. At the Pool, we take tremendous pleasure and pride in sharing their lives with you in *Mark Greschner One Hundred Years of Heart*.

Mayo Schmidt
President and Chief Executive Officer

POOL
TM

INTRODUCTION

Introduction

This book celebrates Saskatchewan's centenarians. In honor of the province's 100th birthday, it pays tribute to men and women who are 100 years of age or older. Some were born here; others arrived as settlers or immigrants. They grew up with the province, farmed its prairie soil, settled its towns, constructed its institutions and developed its traditions. Their lives show the truth of the provincial motto: "From many peoples, strength."

As a professional photographer living in the province's capital, I decided to locate and photograph 100 Saskatchewan people who would be 100 or more years of age in 2005. To my pleasant surprise, I discovered more than 350 centenarians. With the help of the Saskatchewan Centennial Committee, I obtained consent from 180 centenarians who agreed to participate in the project. Throughout 2005, I travelled around the province for photo sessions with them. I recorded our conversations and wrote notes of my impressions. Supplementary information was provided by the centenarians' families, government documents, published biographies, and newspaper and journal articles. In finalizing the text, I tried to ensure accuracy.

Meeting the centenarians gave me a deeper appreciation of our province's character. They spoke to me of hope and heartbreak, of hard work and happy times, and of their satisfaction with lives well-lived. They shared awe in the evolution of technology, a strong sense of community, and a belief in the importance of laughter. They showed me that the heart of this province is its people. The centenarians have inspired me, and I hope their portraits and stories will inspire you.

Eisler, Ursula Anne   Regina
b. April 15, 1905   Odessa, Northwest Territories

The last of seven children, Anne was born in a sod house on the family homestead near Odessa, southwest of Regina. Of her many childhood memories, she recalled burning cow "chips" in the stove. Anne obtained her first driver's licence in 1924 at a cost of $0.75. She and her husband moved to Odessa where they raised a family of eight children. For the past 12 years, Anne has been the Silver Cross Mother at Remembrance Day Services in Regina. Eisler Lake in northern Saskatchewan was named in honour of her son, Leo, who was killed in World War II.

Oystryk, John Yorkton
b. May 14, 1904   Hampton, Northwest Territories

John began his farming career at the age of ten when he was needed to help his father. Over the course of the nearly 60 years that followed, John married, raised three children, continued to operate his own farm, and spent nearly 30 winters in Texas. He felt the best advice he could offer others was to work hard and never complain. "People shouldn't complain," he said. "We live in the greatest province and country."

Bédier, Joe   Hafford
b. November 5, 1905   Manitoba

Few people can take a seemingly mundane activity and turn it into a life-changing event. Apparently, Joe is one of those people. As a young man, he had the task of leading his horses to a watering hole in the bush along a creek. The journey, while necessary, was usually uneventful. But then one day, when he arrived with his horses in tow, a young woman was also there. She and Joe became acquainted and were married in 1939.

Eros, Julia   Spiritwood
b. November 22, 1902   Hungary

Julia was 27 years old when she moved to Canada. The mother of 16 children, Julia was a skilled cook and became well-known for her pea soup. It is a recipe she still continues to make.

Stoeber, Anna M.   Regina
b. July 28, 1900   Northwest Territories

Anna and her husband raised their seven children on their farm north of Vibank. Her son remembered her as a purposeful and organized woman. Well-known in the farming community for her canning expertise, one year Anna prepared over 2,000 containers of canned goods. The advice she always gave her children was to work hard.

Graves, Dorothy H.   Biggar
b. August 13, 1905   Annapolis Valley, Nova Scotia

Dorothy worked in the women's fashion industry in Nova Scotia until getting married in 1925. She and her husband raised four children. After her husband died, Dorothy met Gordon Graves. They were married in 1972 and moved to a farm near Landis. A peaceful woman, Dorothy is fond of animals, particularly the puppies who visit the Lodge where she is currently residing. She still likes to read and appreciates the quietness of sitting outdoors in the sunshine.

Sherdahl, Ralph H. Saskatoon
b. March 12, 1905 Windom, Minnesota

Ralph moved to Canada in 1918 at the age of 13. He married Mabel Ironside in 1931 and the couple raised five children.
Over the years, their family expanded and now includes 12 grandchildren, 14 great-grandchildren, and 1 great-great-grandchild.
Ralph always drove a car and believed the Model T was the best car ever built.

Schroeder, Maria   Battleford
b. August 25, 1905   Austria

Moving from Austria to Canada in 1912, Maria and her family were to sail on the Titanic. They missed its departure by one day.
Following her marriage in 1934, Maria moved to North Battleford where her husband operated a gas station. Active in the life of
her community, Maria was a member of a number of local organizations.

Korchinski, Bernard Leo   Regina
b. December 25, 1905   Beaver Hill, Saskatchewan

Well-read, Bernard conversed with me on topics that ranged from education to politics. An educator by profession, Bernard has also served as a Member of the Saskatchewan Legislative Assembly, a Citizenship Court Judge, and an active member of the Ukrainian community. His has truly been a life devoted to public service.

Thies, Helen Josephine   Churchbridge
b. April 24, 1904   North Dakota

Helen recounted for me the story of the time she was hired to teach in a small country school. As was common in those days, the job included a residence for the teacher and arrangements were made for her to board in a local home. Interestingly, this was also the home of a young man named Paul Thies. In time, the two were married and on their way to raising a family of eight children. A woman of deep and abiding faith, Helen shared these thoughts with me: believe in God, live simply, and work hard. "Hard work never hurt anyone," she added.

Swope, Dirkje   Leoville
b. November 6, 1904   Holland

Full of stories, Dirkje spoke of leaving her native Holland at the age of eight, the excitement of the journey across the Atlantic Ocean, and the incessant bouts of seasickness she had to endure. Her father was a bricklayer who found work building the hospital in North Battleford. Dirkje grew up on the family homestead with her brother and sister, eventually married and raised two children of her own. Educated to Grade Seven, Dirkje was very clear in her advice to others. "Everyone should go to school."

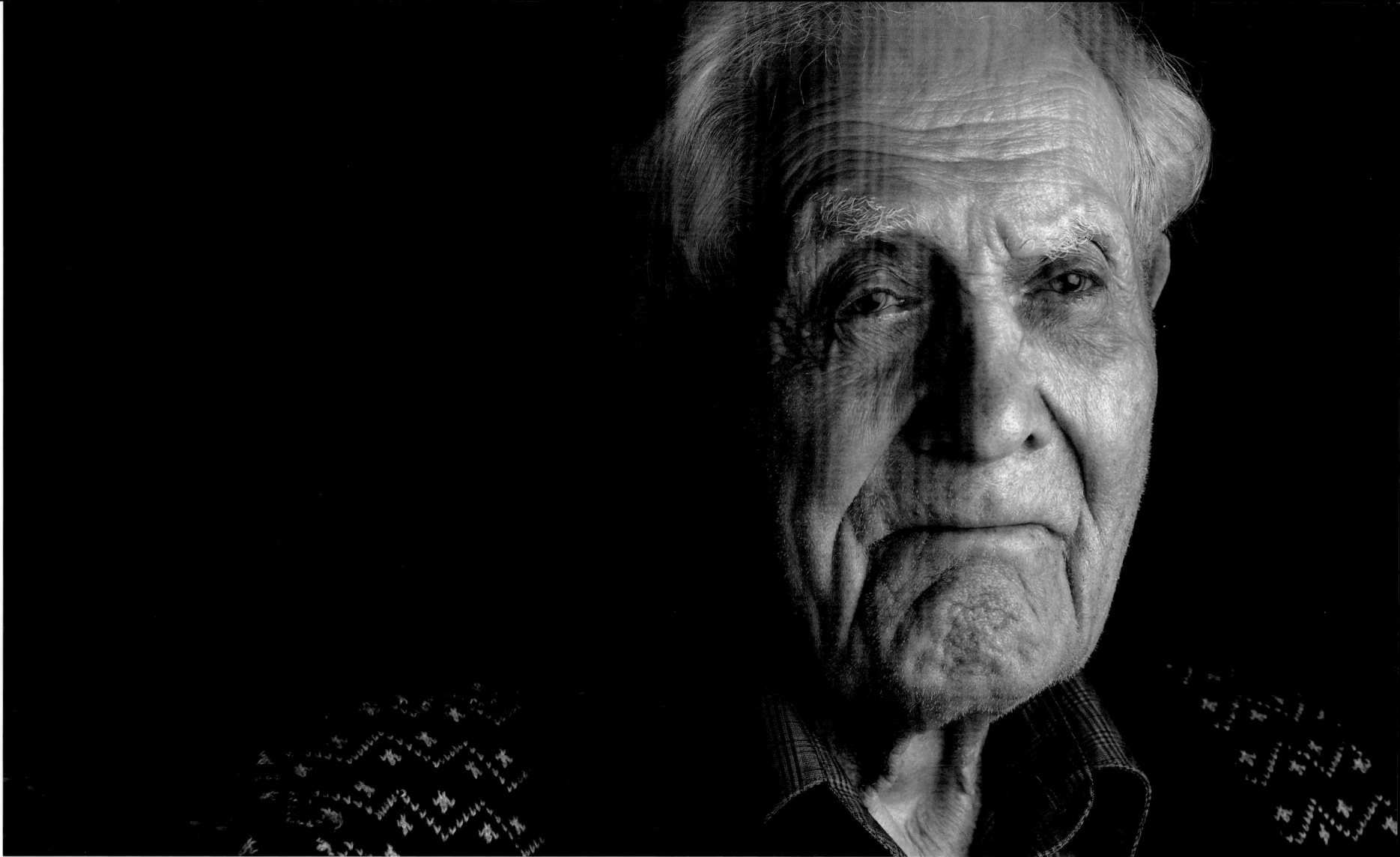

Postle, William H. Warman
b. May 28, 1903 Saskatoon, Northwest Territories

Educated to Grade Seven, Willie left school to farm with his father. Initially working in the fields with horses, he remembered their first tractor, a J.I. Case model. Willie married in 1933 and continued to farm until 1958. Moving to Saskatoon, he took a job as the caretaker at 3rd Avenue United Church. It was a job he held for 17 years. When asked what advice he could share with others, he answered thoughtfully, "Support the churches." The best times in his life have been family celebrations.

Shulko, Annie Kelvington
b. November 30, 1905 Romania

In her community, Annie was known as Grandma Shulko. A wonderful cook who practically lived in her kitchen, she could often been seen out in public wearing her apron. Not afraid of hard work, Annie willingly took on the challenges of farm life. Once, when her husband was delayed on a business trip and the harvest would not wait, she hitched up the horses, enlisted the help of her sons, and set to work swathing the fields of wheat herself. When I had finished photographing Annie, she beckoned me to come nearer so she could deliver a hug and a kiss. It was just what you'd expect from a grandma.

Woitas, Rose   Foam Lake
b. February 1, 1904   Ukraine

Rose was only six weeks old when her family immigrated to Saskatchewan from Ukraine. She married at the age of 16 and, shortly thereafter, settled into farm life on their homestead near Westbend. Raising 16 children on the farm, her life was filled with a great deal of activity, much of it centred in the kitchen.

Farrell, Marion   Regina
b. December 11, 1904   South Shields, England

Growing up in England, Marion's life was touched by World War I in two memorable ways. She vividly recalled the time a German Zeppelin dropped a bomb at the end of her street, completely destroying a children's merry-go-round. When the war ended, Marion's family journeyed to Canada on a former troop ship. As a young woman, she worked as a secretary at Fort San in Fort Qu'Appelle. In time, Marion and her husband moved to Regina, creating a lovely home for their two daughters. She continues to reside in Regina.

Bell, Nellie M.   Regina
b. July 16, 1905   Cottonwood District, Northwest Territories

Nellie has lived her entire life in Saskatchewan. Her family homesteaded on land north of Pense and she recalled growing up there.
In time, she married John William Bell and they moved to Regina where they raised their three daughters. A grandmother to six
grandchildren, Nellie continues to live in Regina.

Hansen, Soren Christian   Saskatoon
b. September 18, 1905   Ullits, Denmark

Soren, his wife, and young daughter moved to Alberta from Denmark in 1953 where arrangements had been made for them to work on a farm. When the farm work was completed, the family moved to Edmonton and Soren spent the winter working in the oilfields at Drayton Valley. After his wife died in 1991, Soren moved to Saskatoon to be near his daughter. While communication is no longer possible for Soren, he loves having people visit with him and continues to be entertained watching hockey games.

Raddatz, Matilda Regina
b. April 11, 1903   Germany

Matilda and her husband, Richard, came to Canada from Germany in 1928 with the dream of owing their own land. Through hard work and perseverance, they were able to purchase some land in 1942 and set to work establishing their own farm. A true pioneer, Matilda faced adversity head-on. When a tornado devastated their farm in 1946, Matilda and her family, with the help of friends and neighbours, simply began again. With life experiences such as this, Matilda's advice for others seemed fitting. "Be happy and enjoy life. Things always work out."

Ranger, Blanche St. Brieux
b. July 27, 1900   Island of Jersey, Brittany

Blanche arrived in Canada with her mother and two siblings in 1910, rejoining her father who had gone ahead of the family in order to establish a homestead. A talented participant in track and field events in her youth, Blanche was educated at the school at Pathlow. Married in 1925, Blanche and her husband raised two sons and two daughters. Evenings on their family farm were often spent listening to the popular radio broadcasts of the time.

Beall, Donna Elizabeth Louise   Saskatoon
b. January 27, 1905   Kinmount, Ontario

Donna graduated from the nursing program at Saskatoon's St. Paul's Hospital in 1926. Her husband was a doctor and together they worked in a number of hospitals across Canada. Donna was delighted when she moved back to Saskatchewan. She always loved the province's expansive sky, the vivid sunsets, and the movement of the wind on fields of wheat in autumn. Reflecting on a century of living, Donna offered this advice; "Work hard. Stand up for what you believe in. Strive to be happy."

Railton, Aline   Indian Head
b. November 14, 1903   Trois-Tistales, Quebec

"I loved young babies, little children, babysitting," Aline told me, her face lighting up. The mother of five, Aline has been fortunate to have a family so willing to accommodate her interests. At last count, the family tally was twenty-one grandchildren, fifty-three great-grandchildren, and twenty-four great-great-grandchildren.

Manz, Johanna V.   Southey
b. April 15, 1904   Illischestie, Bukiowina

When Johanna arrived in Saskatchewan in 1905, her first home was a sod house. As life improved, the family moved into a mud shack with a wooden roof. The wooden house was not built until 1916. Johanna and her brothers and sisters usually walked to school everyday, crossing a set of railroad tracks on the way. The children and the train men saw each other so often, they would wave to each other as the trains passed. Following her marriage in 1924, Johanna and her husband raised six children on their farm.

Friesen, Helen   Saskatoon
b. June 20, 1902   NeuRosenhoff, Ukraine

Helen came to Canada from Ukraine in 1925, spending one year in the province of Ontario. She married and moved to Saskatchewan where she worked on a dairy farm near Dundurn. Throughout her life, Helen enjoyed the music of the piano, playing by note until the age of 95, and thereafter playing by ear. She also took pleasure in needlework and continued to complete needlework projects until the age of 100.

Maguire, Sarah E.   Weyburn
b. September 4, 1904

Sadie celebrated her 100th birthday surrounded by her children, grandchildren, great-grandchildren, and friends. It was an opportunity to reflect on accomplishments made and on challenges bravely faced and overcome. It was a chance to celebrate a life well-lived. Family members shared photographic slides, memories, and talents, making the evening a truly memorable occasion.

Hanson, Palmer R. Spruce Home
b. July 25, 1904 Whitehall, Wisconsin

A genuine man with a wonderful sense of humour, Palmer spoke easily of his life in northern Saskatchewan. He told me of his interest in trapping and shared story after story of his experiences hunting and fishing and of his involvement in clearing the bush north of Prince Albert so that roads could be built. He suggested his longevity was due in large part to his family and good friends. And then he added, "Don't complain. If something comes your way, accept it."

Ziegler, Florantina   Wilkie
b. March 16, 1903   Regina, Northwest Territories

Florantina was working in her garden the evening I arrived to take her photograph. Over a cup of tea and freshly baked cookies, she reminisced about living her entire life in Saskatchewan, and about gardening and fishing, two activities she continues to enjoy. Of the many tips for healthy living she shared with me, one seemed especially important to note: "Don't eat bread that doesn't grow mould."

Haraf, Joseph   Prince Albert
b. April 9, 1903   Krakow, Poland

Joseph arrived in Canada in 1930. Because of the Great Depression, Joseph often did not receive payment for the work
he did on farms. Instead, he worked for room and board. The first farm that employed him was in the Kalyna district.
Following his 1932 marriage, Joseph established a farm at Albertville but eventually returned to the Kalyna area where he
purchased the first farm on which he had worked. When asked the secret to his long life, he suggested it was important to
have a positive attitude, a good sense of humour, and faith. He also liked to have a shot of whiskey every day.

MacLeod, Lora Saskatoon
b. October 1, 1905 Rapid City, Manitoba

Born and raised in Manitoba, Lora's career path has taken many turns. Following the completion of her teacher training at normal school in Winnipeg, Lora taught in a number of schools throughout rural Manitoba. For a brief period of time in the 1930's, she worked for Chatelaine Magazine as a member of the sales staff. By 1937, Lora was working in the seed lab in Winnipeg, a position she held until she transferred to the seed lab in Calgary. Lora married in 1954. Her husband, Ron MacLeod, died in 1977

Lutzko, Pearl   Ituna
b. February 15, 1899   Chortikiw, Ukraine

Running a mixed farm with her husband provided Pearl with space to plant a large garden. It gave her the opportunity to work in the garden all summer and spend autumn days canning her harvest of vegetables. Not surprising, Pearl was a wonderful cook, well-known in her community for her pan-fried potatoes and jelly rolls.

Reiner, Charlotte   Regina
b. December 24, 1900   Czechoslovakia

Born in Czechoslovakia, Charlotte immigrated to Canada at the age of 32 with her husband and two children. A tireless volunteer, Charlotte enjoyed contributing to the work of charities in her community and actively participated in the life of her synagogue.

Plews, Alice M.   Saskatoon
b. October 3, 1903   Ontario

In 1909, Alice's family decided to move to Saskatchewan because her mother had relatives living in the province. Alice recounted stories of growing up in the country. She danced and played the piano and never missed an opportunity to ride horses. "I loved horses," she recalled. Trained as a school teacher, she taught for a time before getting married. When asked the secret to her longevity, she answered, "I enjoyed life!"

Andres, Peter H.   Saskatoon
b. July 22, 1905   Rosthern, Northwest Territories

In his youth, Peter loved sports, playing both baseball and hockey. Following high school, he worked for the government. He enjoyed driving and continued to hold a driver's licence until the age of 97.

Olenchuk, Josephine Big River
b. April 14, 1904 Ukraine

Josephine met her future husband at a Ukrainian dance. Despite having to play the accordion in the band, he managed to ask her to dance three times during the evening. In time, he asked her to marry him. Not one to rush into anything, Josephine waited three years before accepting his proposal. Together, they established a homestead near Big River and raised two sons and a daughter. For Josephine, it was the best time in her life.

Beaumont, Elsie M.   Gull Lake
b. March 14, 1905   Northwest Territories

Many of Elsie 's stories revolved around her family. When I asked her about the worst time in her life, she reflected for a moment and then replied, "the day my daughter got her head stuck in a cream can." After our laughter had subsided, I inquired about the best time in her life. Without hesitation, she answered, "the day I got my daughter's head out of the cream can!" The whole room filled with laughter again.

Rohach, Mary   Prince Albert
b. September 27, 1904   Northwest Territories

Mary grew up on the family homestead near Wakaw. She remembered life on the farm as a time of hard work and recalled ploughing and harrowing the fields using horses. A regular participant at local dances, Mary would often dance "until her feet hurt." Mary has lived her entire life in Saskatchewan. "It is a great place to live," she told me. "The people were and are all so friendly."

Eriksen, Otto Biggar
b. April 23, 1904   Hvalso, Denmark

Otto came to Canada from his native Denmark intending to stay for only two years. He quickly found work on farms and in the bush in northern Alberta. Eventually, he bought his own farm west of Monarch. The farm came fully equipped with a house, barn, horses, and machinery and in no time he had his operation up and running. Married in 1934, Otto and his wife raised five daughters on their farm. While he retired from active farming in 1988, he maintained ownership of the farm until 1994.

Ross, Helena E.   Moose Jaw
b. July 8, 1904   Northwest Territories

Helena's life has been framed by the word "farming". She grew up on a farm, met her future husband at a grain elevator, and helped establish the family farm near Belle Plain. It seemed fitting that when she was asked to describe the best time of her life, Helena replied without hesitation, "living on the farm." Born before the province was incorporated, Helena enjoys telling people that she lived the first part of her life in the Northwest Territories.

Robinson, Florence   Ituna
b. January 30, 1905   Abernethy, Northwest Territories

"Saskatchewan is the greatest place in the world to live," Florence told me. Her stories took her back to the days of living on a mixed farm and of milking cows. She never drove but she remembered seeing "Bennett Buggies" being used in the 1930's by farmers who could not afford gasoline. A telephone operator and store clerk before her marriage, she commented that the best time in her life was when she was married and raising her two children.

Fedorchuk, William   Norquay
b. April 1, 1905   Manitoba

One of the many stories Bill shared with me described a health scare in his youth. At the age of 13, Bill became deathly ill and had to be hospitalized. In an effort to underscore the seriousness of Bill's condition, the doctor offered Bill's father this advice: "You may as well leave him here because he ain't going to make it." Of course, photographing Bill I knew the story had a happy ending and marvelled at how long he'd lived after being so ill. We both laughed trying to imagine how much longer he could live had he always been healthy.

Dobson, Harriet   Regina
b. July 9, 1904   Northwest Territories

Growing up in a home with 12 brothers and sisters, Harriet had plenty of opportunities to put her cooking skills into practice. Her parents loved to dance and they took it upon themselves to teach their children all of their favourite dance steps. Married for more than 70 years, Harriet and her husband raised three children. Her advice to others is to "keep active and eat healthy."

Otto, Daniel Lloydminster
b. February 7, 1905 Zaikimoska, Russia

Arriving in Canada at the age of 23, Daniel had a career in farming that spanned more than 50 years. His farm was located in the Hillmond area. Sociable by nature, Daniel enjoyed dancing and playing cards in the community.

Turnmire, Emma H.   Moosomin
b. April 1, 1903   England

Of the many opportunities that drew immigrants to Canada in the early part of the last century, it was the offer of housekeeping work on prairie farms that brought Emma and her sister to Saskatchewan. Emma reminisced about marrying at the age of 29 on November 29, 1929, raising five children, and enjoying singing and dancing.

Ihle, Kathleen M. Moose Jaw
b. July 13, 1904 England

For Kathleen and her family, the 1930's were a very difficult time. Married and living on the farm, Kathleen worked hard to keep her five children fed and clothed. She maintained a large garden and made all of their clothes by hand.

Simmonds, Dorothy E.   Wadena
b. December 5, 1903

Dorothy has played cards since the age of four. Bridge, whist, and rummy are among her favourite games. At home in the kitchen, she always enjoyed opportunities to bake for her family and friends. Dancing was also an activity she enjoyed throughout her life.

Suignard, Antoine H.   St. Brieux
b. December 1, 1905   Basin Lake District, Saskatchewan

Moving to Canada from France, Antoine was the youngest of six brothers and six sisters. His father built their home on the farm out of logs. It is still standing on the original property. Both Antoine's mother and father possessed a strong religious faith and, as a child, Antoine attended the local church services with them every Sunday.

Ludwig, Mary Antonia   Meadow Lake
b. April 18, 1903   Alameda, Northwest Territories

Moving to Meadow Lake in 1928, Mary and her husband raised 10 children on their farm. While the children were growing up, she tended a large garden and baked bread weekly. For Mary, playing cards was a favourite activity.

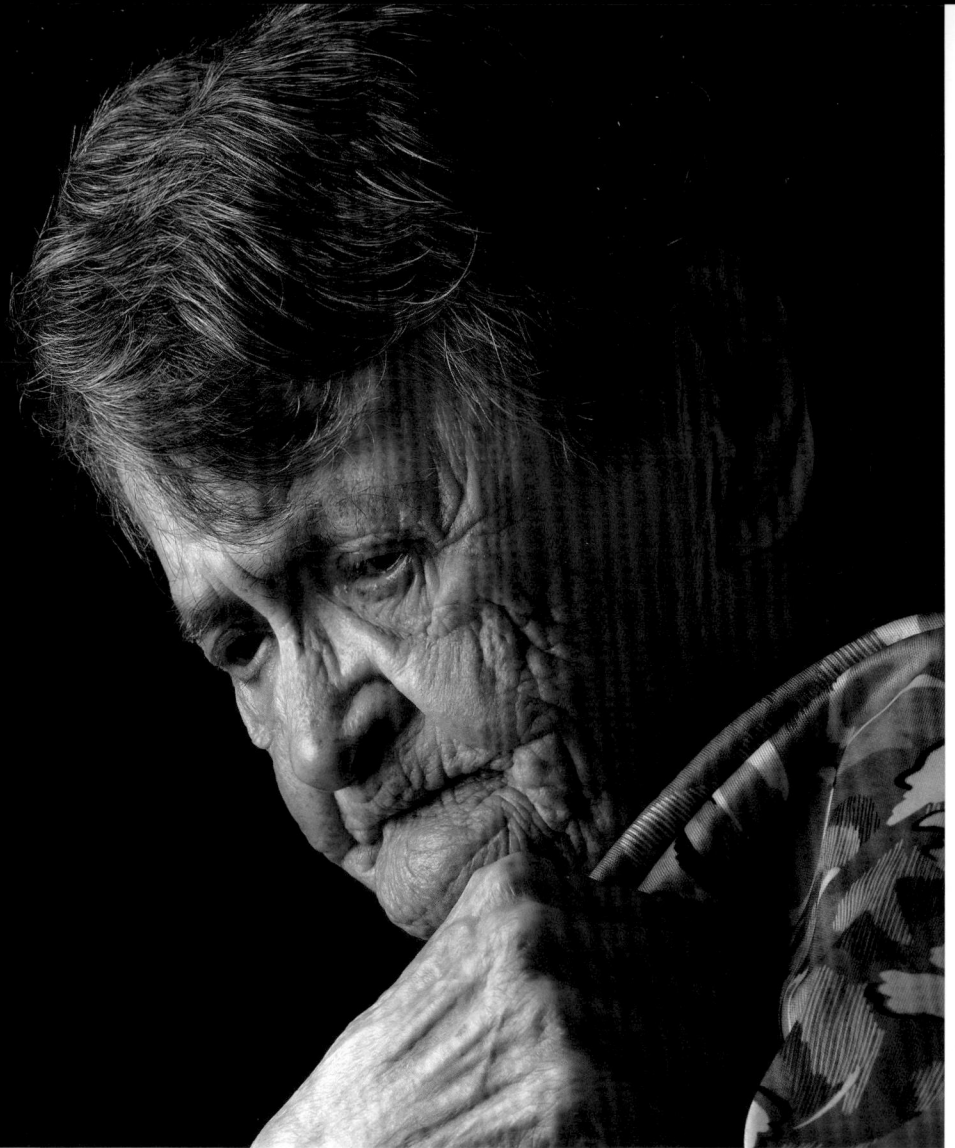

Constantinoff, Wanda   Kerrobert
b. October 5, 1904   Bulgaria

Wanda and her husband established a farm in the Cactus Lake area and it was here where they raised their two sons. Over the course of her life, she has taken pleasure in life on the farm, gardening, singing, walking and spending time with her 11 grandchildren, 22 great-grandchildren, and eight great-great-grandchildren.

Sim, W. Elmer   Saskatoon
b. October 10, 1905   Grenfell, Saskatchewan

Following teachers' college, Elmer taught in a number of schools throughout southern Saskatchewan. He met his future wife while teaching and together they raised three children. Although he left the teaching profession in 1937 to work for the Rural Municipality, his children recalled that the "teacher" in him never completely retired. He continued to correct their spelling and grammar whenever he believed it was necessary. Eager to try new experiences, Elmer took up the game of golf at the age of 50 and was still playing at the age of 98.

Gudmundson, Sigurveig Wynyard
b. August 27, 1905 Winnipegosis, Manitoba

Attending a small rural school two miles south of Wynyard, Veiga's formal education was completed when she reached the end of Grade 8. While growing up on the family farm, Veiga often helped cook for the threshing crews during harvest season. In the process, she became a very good cook. A woman of many talents, Veiga could spin her own wool and knit mittens, socks, and siwash sweaters.

McGill, Margaret O.   Saskatoon
b. July 4, 1904   Minnesota

Following normal school, Margaret began her career as a teacher. One of her first students was Hugh Robertson. He went on to become a leading health care provider in Saskatchewan. When the Provincial Laboratories were renamed in his honour, he made mention of the influence Margaret's teaching had on his life. Margaret and her husband shared an interest in gardening. As a member of the Saskatoon Horticultural Society, Margaret was consistently recognized for her beautiful petunias. She became known as the "Petunia Queen".

Veitch, James   Saskatoon
b. February 15, 1901   Peebles, Scotland

James came to Canada with his grandparents and lived with them on a farm in the Bruno area. Growing up, he repeatedly asked his grandfather for a violin. Eventually, his grandfather granted his request. Having the ability to play music by ear, James played every weekend at local dances. As an adult, James worked as a plumber and became part of Smith Plumbing, a company still operating today. His daughter fondly remembered spending summers fishing with him at Christopher Lake.

Boyle, Anna   Dodsland
b. January 15, 1905   Insinger, Northwest Territories

Anna had such a positive energy about her, just talking to her made me smile. Her stories ranged from growing up on the farm and going to school to raising her own children and her interest in cooking, sewing, and quilting. When asked what advice she could offer others based on her life experiences, she remarked, "Work hard and be honest."

Swedberg, Helen   Big River
b. April 1, 1904   Kansas

Helen married the "boy next door", her husband having grown up on the neighbouring farm. Together they raised five children on their farm in the Yorkton area. Helen believed the years she spent raising her young family were the best years of her life.

Mortin, Ernest C.   Saskatoon
b. July 2, 1905   Ontario

"The best year of my life was 1936," Ernest told me. Crops were good. He was hired to work as a grain buyer for the North Star Grain Company, making a monthly income of $50.00. It was also the year he got married. When North Star could not afford to employ him the following year, the Saskatchewan Wheat Pool hired him. It was an association that lasted 25 years. When I asked him the secret to his long life, he refused to share it with me. "I'll sell it to you," he laughed. It may have something to do with genetics. His father lived to the age of 90.

Baumung, Elizabeth   Langenburg
b. Sept. 12, 1904   Northwest Territories

While talking to Elizabeth and learning about her interests, it became apparent that she was a woman who understood the importance of having beauty and joy in one's life. Elizabeth wrote poetry and played the mandolin. A faithful gardener, her flowers flourished under her care. It was the same nurturing environment in which Elizabeth and her husband raised their three sons and two daughters.

Cornell, Doris Lilian   North Battleford
b. August 21, 1904

Farm life in the early days of the province was often quite isolated. So it was not surprising when Doris revealed to me that she did not even see a car until the age of 14. The late introduction to the world of transportation did not seem to have a lasting effect, however. Doris loved to travel and continued to drive her Volkswagen Beetle until 1990. Her grandchildren still drive her car. Doris also enjoyed fishing, an activity introduced to her by her husband.

Curle, Marion   Redvers
b. March 6, 1904   Prince Edward Island

As a young woman, Marion had an interest in a number of sports, including hockey and skating. A trained educator, she taught school in Saskatchewan from 1922 to 1932. Following her marriage, her interests turned to gardening, dancing, and the raising of her four children. She is still a devoted fan of the game of hockey.

Croteau, Marie Sr.   Prince Albert
b. January 3, 1905   St. John, North Dakota

Sister Marie's family moved to Canada from North Dakota because the land was available and affordable. A teacher, Sister Marie
joined the Sisters of the Presentation of Mary at the age of 20. She continued to teach Grade Five and Six students in a number of
northern communities in the province for 33 years. Following her retirement from teaching, Sister Marie worked as a seamstress at
the convent. She continues to live at the convent in Prince Albert.

Plumb, Reginald   Saskatoon
b. October 30, 1903   Ontario

Visiting with Reginald was special. He still lived on his own and our conversation ranged from his memories of his wife to his 49 year association with Famous Players Theatres. Reginald began his career in Saskatoon at the Daylite Theatre, working the night shift for $1.00 a night. By 1929, he had taken on the role of assistant manager at the newly constructed Capital Theatre. The opening show at the theatre was one of the first talking movies. Interested in a number of sports throughout his life, Reginald proudly described achieving a score of 76 in a golf game played at the age of 76.

Platz, Arrie North Battleford
b. March 3, 1903 United States of America

The second oldest of 12 children, Arrie helped her father with the bulk of the farm chores. Attending country schools, she played baseball and loved going to dances. As a young woman, she moved to North Battleford where she found work as a seamstress and yard goods clerk in a store. In the 41 years she was employed at the store, Arrie never missed a day of work due to illness. Arrie enjoyed driving and recalled that the first car she owned was an Austin. She paid $100.00 for it.

Wells, Harold   Saskatoon
b. August 3, 1904   South Coast, England

At the age of seven, Harold moved to the Weyburn area with his family. One of his early memories was of his mother selling butter once a week for groceries. Harold enjoyed cars. His favourite car was a Thunderbird and he recalled the story of buying the car in Montreal and then driving it home to Saskatchewan. Young adulthood was remembered as a highlight of his life.

Wolf, Esther   Biggar
b. July 24, 1900   Dayton, Ohio

Esther's family homesteaded in the Swarthmore region. After she married in 1920, she and her husband established their own farm.
Dedicated and tireless, she assisted her husband in the operation of the farm and raised the couple's three children. When time
allowed, Esther played the piano. It is an activity she still continues to enjoy.

Teichroeb, Daniel P.   Saskatoon
b. April 20, 1904   South Russia

Daniel moved to Canada in 1924 and found work as a farmhand in the Warman area. He married in 1926, and he and his
wife raised six children on their own farm. Daniel continued to farm until 1950 and then worked for a time with a bricklayer.
His favourite leisure activities include watching sporting events and movies.

Harlos, Margaret   Regina
b. June 1, 1902   Austria

Immigrating to Saskatchewan from Austria, Margaret and her family settled in the Govan area. Marrying in 1917, she and her husband established their own farm near Avonhurst. There they raised two children. An active woman, Margaret enjoyed participating in the dances held in her community.

Fry, Gladys Ellen   Cupar
b. June 11, 1905   Regina, Northwest Territories

After they married in 1923, Gladys and her husband operated a mixed farm. A large garden and the animals raised on the farm provided for their needs and before long their family had grown to 11 children. Gladys had a camera and she delighted in taking photographs of the family and life on the farm, often using the money she earned from selling cream to cover the cost of film developing. Gladys loved completing crossword puzzles. It was an activity that continued to entertain her well into her 90's.

Lyell, Catherine   Saskatoon
b. April 9, 1905   Ethelbert, Manitoba

Catherine recounted for me a childhood adventure. One day, she made her way to the pasture to collect the milk cows. Noticing the bull also out in the field, Catherine suddenly had a wonderful idea. In a matter of minutes, she was resting on the back of the bull and looking forward to an entertaining ride around the field. Unknown to Catherine, the bull had plans of his own. Without warning, the bull charged across the field toward a group of willow bushes. While thrilling, the ride was short-lived. Catherine was knocked to the ground by the willows, ending what might have been a promising bull-riding career.

Steeves, Agnes I.   Carievale
b. July 30, 1905   Norma, North Dakota

A frequent traveller, Agnes loved to drive. When her grandchildren reached the driving age, she took on the role of driving
instructor. Agnes continued to maintain her own driver's licence until she was 93. An active volunteer in her community,
Agnes also danced and wrote poetry.

Volman, Theresa   Regina
b. February 11, 1902   Herczegfalva/Mezfalva Fejer, Hungary

Theresa married in 1918 and moved with her husband to a farm south of Lestock. She remembered teams of horses being used
in the fields to help with the work of farming. Her days on the farm were filled with the activities that accompany the feeding and
clothing of 12 children. At the age of 65, Theresa and her husband retired from farming and moved to Regina where she continues
to reside.

Allen, Elsie Mildred   Regina
b. April 23, 1905   Caledonia Township, Ontario

Elsie shared stories of growing up with her four sisters on the family farm. As a young woman, she and her sisters loved dancing and regularly attended the local dances. Skilled in the intricacies of square dancing, Elsie and her sisters became very popular dance partners. An independent woman, Elsie continued to live in her own apartment until 2002.

Lutzer, Gustav   Regina
b. August 29, 1902   Kurgany, Ukraine

A man devoted to God, Gustav believes it is his strong faith that led him through the many sorrows and challenges he has faced in life. At the age of seven, he went to work for a family when his own family could no longer provide for him. Gustav was deported to Afghanistan at the outbreak of World War I, a period when many of his family members, including his mother, perished. Finally, at the age of 26, he moved to Saskatchewan. After working on several farms in the province, he established his own farm in the Colfax area, married, and raised a family. For Gustav, Saskatchewan truly was a land of opportunity.

Piche, Blanche   Gravelbourg
b. November 9, 1904   Belcourt, North Dakota

A native of North Dakota, Blanche moved to Canada with her family in 1913. She and her family settled on a farm north of Lafleche.

Erickson, Helen   Kyle
b. August 9, 1902   Bessarrabia, Russia

Helen's formal education ended at Grade Four when she was pressed into service helping her mother look after the people who were boarding at their home. As a young woman, Helen found work packaging cookies and dipping chocolates. Married in Winnipeg, she and her husband had a daughter. When her husband died, Helen and her daughter travelled to Sanctuary, Saskatchewan to help her sister. Helen met and married the cook at the Sanctuary Hotel and before long the two had bought the hotel. Helen continued to dip chocolates as a hobby and also pursued her interest in knitting, sewing, and embroidery.

McLeod, Clara G.   Radville
b. July 20, 1905   North Dakota

When I asked Clara to tell me stories of her life, she replied with a laugh, "Do they have to be true?" Then she related this tale. One day walking home from school, Clara was chased by a bull. She saw her refuge on the other side of a fence and ran toward it. Just as she rolled under the fence, the bull charged directly into the fence. "Not much of a story," she explained, "but it's true." For Clara, the best time in her life was when she was teaching. Knowing she would have to resign from teaching when she married in 1926, Clara and her husband kept their marriage secret so she could remain teaching one more year.

Miller, Ella   Langenburg
b. March 4, 1904   Manitoba

Ella was born into a very musical family. Both her mother and father played musical instruments so it was not surprising that Ella often played piano in a band. Ella also loved to dance and regularly attended the dances in her community. She worked as a telephone operator and it was a time in her life she remembered with fondness. "People were more friendly then," she noted.

Giesbrecht, Anna Swift Current
b. June 25, 1905   Neuenburg, Manitoba

Anna attended a small school in Hamburg, a village not far from McMahon. It was a German school and she recalled her studies focusing mainly on the Bible and on arithmetic. One of her favourite activities in school was preparing for the annual Christmas programs. Anna's wedding took place on February 13, 1927. Being quiet and shy by nature, she maintains it was a day she did not enjoy. Her husband died in 1970 and a few years later she met and married John Giesbrecht.

Scott, Alta B.   Rosetown
b. December 5, 1902   Barnes, Oklahoma

Alta and her family moved to Canada to take advantage of the offer of affordable land. Unfortunately, their original homestead in the Wascana Flats district had to be abandoned because all but ten acres was covered by water. By 1905, the family had moved to their new homestead south of Venn. Married in 1928, Alta and her husband set up their own farm and raised three children. Although her husband died in 1955, she continued to run the farm until 1959. At that time, she married Dunning Scott and the couple moved to Saskatoon. There they opened Dunn Scott Realty and Alta began a new career as office manager.

Basaraba, Fredrick J.   Lanigan
b. March 7, 1904   North Dakota

The second oldest of ten children, Fred was raised on the family farm. In time he married and opened a small general store and post office. Eventually, the pull of farm life was stronger than his interest in the store and he returned to running a farm south of Saskatoon. Extremely involved in the life and work of his community, Bob was an active member of the Rural Municipality and the Hospital Board.

Robertson, Leva May   Fort Qu'Appelle
b. August 8, 1902   Springbrook, Northwest Territories

The middle of ten children, May was raised on the family farm in the Qu'Appelle region. As an adult, she clerked in the Red and White store in her community and was very active in her church. May delighted in working on a variety of crafts, particularly embroidery. She was a dedicated gardener. Devoted to her family, May cared for both her parents in their later years.

McCormick, Solveig   Moose Jaw
b. May 17, 1901   Norway

"She has always been a very independent lady," Solveig's daughter told me. Coming to Canada in 1906, Solveig and her sister were sent to live with an aunt. Over the next few years, the girls lived with families in Kennedy and Regina. Somewhere along the way, the sisters were separated. Thirty-four years passed before Solveig saw her sister again.

Larionyk, Tekla   Saskatoon
b. August 3, 1905   Village of Kremediv, Ukraine

During our conversation, Tekla remarked that her fondest memories were of being married and raising her young family on the farm. She kept an expansive garden and reaped its benefits every autumn. A great cook, her family was always well-fed. In addition to knitting and cross-stitching, Tekla took a great deal of pleasure in reciting poetry and singing.

Haddow, Peter D. H.   Saskatoon, Saskatchewan
b. November 1, 1904   Scotland

So full of life and humour, it was a pleasure spending time with Peter. Coming to Canada at the age of 20, Peter became a chef at the Bessborough Hotel in Saskatoon. He enjoyed playing soccer and it was at a soccer match that he met his future wife. It turned out she was the hotel manager's daughter. They married and had three children. Peter never learned to drive a car, preferring instead to walk everywhere. He continues to walk two miles every day. When I asked if he ever smoked, Peter replied," Yes, but my doctor told me to quit because it wasn't good for me." "When did you quit," I inquired further. "Last year," he laughed.

Schuster, Martha   Regina
b. April 19, 1904   Wolseley, Northwest Territories

In her youth, Martha enjoyed the autumn harvests when the job of threshing was accomplished with the help of horses. Her passion was raising chickens, ducks, and turkeys. She also maintained lovely gardens. After moving to Southey in 1978, she became known for the beautiful flower arrangements she would donate to local churches. A great fan of curling, Martha continued to participate in curling games until she was 85 years of age.

Melton, Florence   Estevan
b. November 30, 1905   Carnduff, Saskatchewan

Florence was born on the family farm north-west of Carnduff. According to her family, Florence recalled the days of prohibition and instances of "Rum Runners" racing across her farm property. Trained as a teacher, Florence taught in a number of rural one-room schools. Some of the schools, like M & S Mines School, were built by mining companies.   Her career as a teacher lasted more than 40 years. Following her retirement, Florence and her sister travelled extensively across Canada and throughout Great Britain.

Shields, Robert   Wood Mountain
b. October 1904   Culbertson, Manitoba

Bob was skilled in electronics and for a time operated his own radio station in Wood Mountain. Since it was not a properly licensed station, Bob had to avoid detection by the radio licensing authorities by broadcasting his programs at a variety of radio frequencies. Eventually, he was identified and his station was shut down. A man of independence, Bob continued to live on his own until the age of 99.

Ward, Robert Phillip Regina
b. December 31, 1905 Portage la Prairie, Manitoba

Full of energy, having a conversation with Phillip was a blast! He loved to cook, having been taught in his youth by his mother. An avid baseball player throughout his life, he shared wonderful stories of the game. He also spoke of his enjoyment of curling and dancing, two activities in which he still participates on a regular basis. A man who lives his own advice, Phillip counselled me, "Eat properly and keep moving."

Kirby, Gladys M.   Rockglen
b. August 16, 1903   Kansas

Gladys lived in her own home until the age of 99. Always eager for a visit, she was a familiar sight at the senior's drop in centre in her community. Gladys loved to work on puzzles or participate in a game of cards. Rummy was a game she particularly enjoyed.

Sweeney, Edna B.   Bengough
b. June 19, 1904   Cooperstown, North Dakota

The youngest daughter in a family of 11 children, Edna's formal education ended at the beginning of high school when her mother died. Edna was 14 years old and stayed home to look after her brothers. A very musical family, two of her brothers played in a band. Edna learned to play the violin, an instrument she continues to play. Moving to a mixed farm following her wedding, Edna's life was filled with knitting, crocheting, writing poetry, and the joys and challenges of raising seven children. When asked to identify the best time of her life, Edna remarked that her whole life has been the best time.

Dalgleish, Marion K.   Saskatoon
b. February 1, 1905   Medicine Hat, Northwest Territories

Growing up the only girl in a family of boys taught Marion some important life lessons. "I learned how to fight!" Not surprising, school and school dances became the centre of her social life. A teacher in small rural schools, Marion recalled the challenges of educating 43 students in her class. When her father died, Marion left the teaching profession and took over the running of the farm. She never learned to drive a car. "I never needed to learn. There were always lots of young men around to give me a ride," she laughed.

Swick, Molly   Prince Albert
b. November 3, 1904   St. Julien, Northwest Territories

Molly was born in the village of St. Julien, near the town of Wakaw. She grew up in the Wakaw area and after she married, ran the post office and a business. She and her husband had two sons.

McKenty, Margareet, Regina
b. December 22, 1902 Rossland, British Columbia

Margareet's family moved to a farm south of Broadview in 1911. Her mother died when she was eight years old. When a farming accident claimed the life of her father in 1916, Margareet moved into Regina. It was a period she remembered as the worst time in her life. Margareet found employment as a file clerk with the Simpson's department store. When asked about her life, she commented, "It's too long."

Kozoriz, Mary   Tisdale
b. July 1, 1904   Ukraine

Born in Ukraine, eight month old Mary and her family journeyed to Canada on a cattle boat. Raised on the family farm
at Wakaw, Mary was no stranger to hard work. When her mother became ill, Mary took on the bulk of the housework.
She was five years old at the time. Mary recollected stories of tending the garden and of sewing using the cloth of flour
sacks. Not having the opportunity to attend school, she taught herself English.

Petro, Katherine   Swift Current
b. September 15, 1904   La Lehr, North Dakota

Katherine spent her childhood on the family farm south of Maple Creek. In her youth, Katherine and her sister had the task of tending the cattle. Distracted one day, they began to play a game of tag around a large boulder out in the field. As they did this, the cattle wandered away. A neighbour came upon the scene and, seeing what he thought were a couple of coyotes playing around the boulder, fired a shot at the girls. Katherine and her sister screamed. The story concluded with the neighbour taking the girls home and then retrieving the cattle. As an adult, Katherine was very active in the life and work of her community.

Johnson, Margaret   Denholm
b. December 24, 1905   Garland, Manitoba

Maggie and her husband operated a mixed farm north of Denholm. She always planted a large garden on the farm and her daughters remember helping her with the weeding. A good cook, Maggie often sent the children off to school with peanut butter sandwiches made on her freshly baked bread. Special foods, like fried carrots and a Norwegian potato dish, were always reserved for holiday meals. According to her family, Maggie's fondest memories have been of fishing at La Ronge and of family gatherings. Her advice to her family has always been to work hard and be happy.

Malfair, Agnes   Carrot River
b. April 15, 1905   St. Louis, Northwest Territories

According to her daughter, Agnes loved the space of the prairies. Married at the age of 17, Agnes and her husband set up a farm at Rosthern. Despite the work of running a farm, raising nine children, and the seemingly never-ending cooking duties, Agnes still found time for the activities she loved: working in her garden, socializing, and playing cards.

Wickstrom, Inez   Cabri
b. January 18, 1905   Shequidah, Manitoulen Island, Ontario

A woman dedicated to her community, Inez was an active member of the local school and library boards. Associated with the Credit Union for a number of years, she was recognized as the first woman in Canada to head a credit union with assets of over one million dollars. Inez still enjoys visiting with young people and always encourages them to follow their interests, develop their talents, and continue learning.

Macpherson, Helen M.   Wawota
b. March 12, 1904   Scotland

"The best time of my life," Helen told me, "was when I was married with a young family." Married in 1925, Helen and her husband raised four children. After her husband died in 1968, Helen took on the occasional babysitting job. One of the families she looked after was that of Allan Blakeney, the Premier of Saskatchewan from 1971-1982. Helen believes her long life can be attributed to her diet. She confided that she eats one egg every morning, does not eat meat, and consumes plenty of vegetables. "Yams are good for you," she added.

Love, Hazel   Saskatoon
b. August 19, 1905   Moorhead, Minnesota

Hazel married Samuel Love in 1943. He was the funeral director in Wadena and following their marriage, Hazel joined him in operating Love's Funeral Home. She enjoyed pastimes that allowed her to work with her hands. Hazel worked in her garden and tended her flower beds. A talented seamstress, she produced lovely needlepoint. Equally skilled in the kitchen, Hazel loved to bake.

Matz, Laura M.   Christopher Lake
b. April 20, 1905   Shellbrook, Northwest Territories

Laura said little during her photo session until the topic of her career arose. Married to a farmer, Laura had been employed as a teacher in small country schools. She recalled the activities involved in the teaching of the children in those classrooms providing her with some of the best experiences of her life.

Garth, Mabel   Langham
b. January 5, 1904   Belfast, Ireland

I enjoyed chatting with Mabel. High-spirited and full of fun, she shared with me stories of arriving in Canada at the age of five and of growing up on the family homestead near Cutknife. Remaining in the Cutknife area following her marriage, Mabel assisted her husband on their farm and raised their three children. Working in her large garden was one of her favourite diversions.

Potter, Amy I.   Rabbit Lake
b. September 2, 1904   Manitoba

Because of her failed hearing, our conversation consisted of me writing questions on paper and Amy entertaining me with her stories and advice. "Read as much as you can," she suggested. "Laugh more. The world needs more laughter." Then with a hint of mischief twinkling in her eyes she grinned, "Only the good die young".

Holowenko, Julia   Hudson Bay
b. August 16, 1901   Bukovina Region of Ukraine

Born in Ukraine, Julia came to Canada when she was nine years old. Married at the age of 16, she and her husband bought
a homestead near Hudson Bay for $10.00. A tireless worker, Julia fed and clothed her children, tended the livestock on
the farm, sold produce grown in her garden, maintained a trap line, and made rag rugs to sell in town. With her grandson
translating, she spoke to me in Ukrainian of her love of music and dancing, and of the accordion, an instrument she still
plays "when her hands are feeling good."

Pankoski, Mary   Yorkton
b. November 19, 1903   Kilally, Northwest Territories

In 1922, Mary married Howard Pankoski and together they farmed until 1953. Following their retirement, they moved to Jedburgh and ran the hotel. After her husband's death in 1959, Mary continued to operate the hotel herself. She retired in 1968 and moved to Yorkton. For her family, Mary's strength of character has been a continual source of inspiration.

Austen, Bruno   Middle Lake
b. July 1, 1905   Sussenberg, Germany

Bruno explained to me that he came to Canada from Germany at the age of 21 in search of a better life. He appreciated the "space of the land" in Saskatchewan and while immigrant life was not easy, he was determined to make it work. Eventually he established a farm in the Middle Lake district. When asked what he considered the best thing in his life, Bruno paused briefly and then responded, "being married to my wife." Sitting just off to Bruno's side, out of camera range, his wife of 60 years quietly wiped a tear from her eye.

Messenger, Susan Kelvington
b. January 23, 1905   Esterhazy, Northwest Territories

Susan is dedicated to gardening. Every February, while her garden is still buried under a blanket of snow, she starts her flowers indoors. When the time is right, she moves them to her own little greenhouse and eventually out into the garden. Not surprising, her flowers flourish under such attention. Susan continues to live in her own home and play cards when the opportunity arises. She still likes to walk. "I have walked all my life."

Waterhouse, E. Mabel   Paynton
b. June 3, 1905   Bresaylor, Northwest Territories

Mabel loves to listen to the birds outside her window. She stocks a large bird feeder to give them a meeting place and talks to any bird that stays around long enough to listen. On the day I visited Mabel, she informed one such bird, "The old lady's still here!" Mabel's advice to others is to keep busy and it seems to suit her own life very well. She remains interested in gardening and cooking. For many years, Mabel reserved every Victoria Day weekend for camping with her family. It was a tradition that ended when she reached the age of 96.

Doyle, Winnifred   Regina
b. October 27, 1905   Doght, Ireland

Our conversation centred on Winnifred's move from Ireland to Saskatchewan at the age of 18, on her life in Regina and on her family. One of her fondest memories was of taking her children to Wascana Lake for a swim on hot summer days. When asked the secret to a long life, she advised, "Don't smoke or drink and never worry."

Romaniuk, Edith   Yorkton
b. November 10, 1905   Donwell, Saskatchewan

Edith and her husband operated a farm south-east of Gorlitz. A generous woman, Edith delighted in sharing with others the vegetables produced in her garden. She also enjoyed creating crocheted Afghan blankets for family and friends. The couple's son, Danny, rose to prominence in Canada as a country music musician. An award, named in his honour, is presented annually to musicians in British Columbia who make outstanding contributions to country music. Edith's niece, Sylvia Fedoruk, was Saskatchewan's first female Lieutenant Governor.

Hoffer, Alma K.   Saskatoon
b. January 24, 1905   Laird, Northwest Territories

Alma recalled a childhood of working hard on the farm. Not the sort of person to normally get into trouble, she remembered being at the supper table and her dad giving her a tap on the head with a broomstick whenever he felt she needed it. On the day that I photographed her, Alma sat in a rocking chair that was over 150 years old. The chair had a special significance for her. It had belonged to her mother.

Epp, Lydia   Saskatoon
b. June 15, 1905   Germany

Coming to Canada in 1949, Lydia was an energetic worker. During the day, she held a job doing housework and at night she cleaned grain. When she wasn't working, crocheting and knitting were two activities she enjoyed.

Ryan, Ole A.   Midale
b. December 19, 1901   Sparbu, Norway

Arriving in Canada in 1907, Ole's father established a homestead south of Outram. Ole grew up helping his father on the farm and eventually took over the running of the farm as a young man. Married in 1933, Ole and his wife raised three children. With his retirement from farming in 1957, his interest turned to music. Having played the violin all of his life, he began to devote his time to the making of violins. Over the years he has created a total of four. Known as a man who always had a joke to share, Ole has truly enjoyed life. When asked his advice for others, he offered, "Live your life honestly."

Ronsman, Jules Tyvan
b. July, 12 1905 Belgium

Jules' daughter, who accompanied him to the photo session, shared with me stories of her father's life. Educated to Grade Six, Jules was a hard worker. Establishing a mixed farm in the Tyvan area, he continued farming into his 70's. A lifelong trapper, Jules was also a talented woodworker. He was particularly skilled in creating wooden models of farm machinery, buggies, and wagons.

Rolph, Nettie   Melfort
b. May 7, 1903   Manitoba

Nettie loved to dance, particularly to the music of the big bands. Married three times during the course of her life, she raised one son. Nettie identified her marriages as the best times in her life. "Everyone should be married," she advised.

Gomersall, William G.   Moose Jaw
b. March 21, 1905   Huntley, Ontario

Known as the "last Saskatchewan cowboy", Bill continues to reside on the ranch he purchased in the 1930's. He shared stories with me of his love of horses and of working with them as a young boy. A respected horse trainer, Bill earned a reputation as a rancher dedicated to, and proficient in, the raising of rodeo stock. While retirement has not slowed the pace of life for Bill, it has allowed him to indulge in his other passion. He delights in reciting poetry at cowboy poetry festivals throughout southern Saskatchewan.

Mann, Ruby   Saskatoon
b. August 28, 1904

A school teacher as a young adult, Ruby shared with me stories of her husband and two sons, of life on the farm, and of her love of dancing. When asked to describe the best time of her life, she thought for a moment and replied that she had lived a life "filled with good times."

Vandermeulen, Agnes   Regina
b. October 6, 1900   Boscurivs, Northwest Territories

In the early days of education in the province, women were allowed to teach as long as they remained unmarried. While Agnes enjoyed her work as a teacher, her engagement at the age of 24 signalled the end of her career. She and her husband settled on a farm in the Yorkton area where they raised two children. Of the stories Agnes shared with me, one seemed truly remarkable. Over the course of her entire life, she was never hospitalized due to illness.

Zawislak, Annie   Canora
b. December 28, 1905   Hazel Dell, Saskatchewan

Annie was born and raised in the eastern part of the province. A childhood of working on the farm left little opportunity for formal education and so, as an adult, Annie learned English from her 13 children. Skilled in the kitchen, Annie's favourite meal was cabbage rolls with buckwheat perogies.

Erickson, Carl   Shell Lake
b. December 9, 1903   South Dakota

Carl moved to Saskatchewan from South Dakota at the age of seven and never left. A kind and gentle man, he spoke of his enjoyment of fishing and curling, and of playing in an orchestra with his brothers. His greatest joy has been the life he has shared with his wife for over 70 years.

Haufe, Hedy   St. Walburg
b. October 21, 1905   Austria

Born in Austria, Hedy and her husband moved to Saskatchewan in 1939. Obtaining land, they pursued their interest in farming.
When they retired from farming in 1955, they moved to St. Walburg where Hedy worked in the hospital.

Bowler, Percy Gravelbourg
b. August 23, 1900   Llanhister, Wales

Immigrating to Saskatchewan in 1911, Percy's family obtained land near Gravelbourg and began settling into life on the farm. A classical music teacher, Percy's mother made sure the children had opportunities to be involved in music. In Percy's case, that meant learning to play the violin, piano, and organ. A bachelor, he made a career of farming and regularly participated in the social activities that were organized throughout the Gravelbourg community.

Dubyk, Ksenka   Saskatoon
b. August 5, 1904   Ukraine

Ksenka's parents sent her to Canada at the age of 25 to find work and make a little money. She lived with her aunt in a village near Wakaw. When she married, she moved with her husband to North Battleford where they raised six children. A devout woman, Ksenka continues to read scripture in Ukrainian. She attributes her long life to her belief in God. "He has been taking care of me," she added.

Kungle, Ignace   Wakaw
b. January 19, 1904   Wakaw, Northwest Territories

Ignace was a very talented musician. He played the accordion, violin, and drums. A much sought after band member, his musical groups played at dances throughout the Wakaw area. He played baseball in his youth and participated in bird hunting. He was still fishing at the age of 86. One of Ignace's favourite endeavours was painting buildings. He last gave his barn a coat of paint when he was 95 years old.

Karapita, Margaret Regina
b. December 19, 1905 Regina, Saskatchewan

Born into a family of ten, Margaret grew up in a sod house on the family farm south of Regina. One of her early memories of life on the farm was of her father breaking land with oxen. She spoke of her wedding in August 1929. "It was a hot day on the farm," she recalled. Margaret and her husband raised three children. One of her favourite pastimes has been playing cards.

Marvin, Jonasina Valla   Langenburg
b. September 12, 1903   Sinclair, Manitoba

After attending normal school in Moosomin, Valla taught near the community of Churchbridge. There she met and married Harvey Marvin and they established a farm in the Churchbridge region. A very active member of the community, Valla enjoyed the opportunities for leadership that community projects and events provided. She also loved to sing. Valla attributes her longevity to staying active and maintaining a positive outlook on life. She also believes her keen interest in the well-being of her family and friends has played an important role.

Hunt, Ivy   Rosetown
b. March 31, 1905   Dinnington, County York, England

Within two years of moving to Canada, Ivy's family was farming in the Kenaston area. By 1912, they had moved to Regina where they lived in a sod house and Ivy attended school. As a young adult, Ivy held a number of jobs. She was a housekeeper for a time in Saskatoon and also worked as a cook on farms during the fall harvests. It was during one of her harvest cook jobs that she met her future husband. After they married, Ivy and her husband moved to a farm near Sovereign and Ivy settled into the rhythm of farm life. An avid gardener, Ivy often received recognition for her beautiful flowers and well-kept yard.

Ehrmantraut, Mary Estevan
b. March 19, 1905   Estevan, Northwest Territories

Mary shared with me her memories of living in the south-eastern part of the province. Growing up on the family farm near Estevan, Mary recalled her formal education ending at Grade Seven. She enjoyed participating in some sports in her youth and learned to play the piano. Attending a dance one evening, Mary met the man who would become her husband. Together, they raised a family that eventually included six children.

Madey, Gertrude   Wynyard
b. February 2, 1898   Wynyard, Northwest Territories

An energetic woman, Gertrude raised seven children on the family farm. Often her days would be filled assisting her husband in farming activities with the evenings reserved for housekeeping duties.

Carriere, Frances Saskatoon
b. August 3, 1904   New York City, New York

"I love the climate in Saskatchewan," Frances told me during our photo session. Throughout her life, she pursued activities that gave her opportunities to be outdoors. Chief among these activities have been gardening and walking. Very musical, Frances expressed her delight in playing the piano and in dancing. When asked her advice for a good life, Frances replied, "Eat well and be honest."

Wasyluk, Mike   Wynyard
b. April 5, 1905   Ukraine

The oldest of 13 children, Mike came to Canada in 1907. An industrious worker, he farmed in the Parkerview area of the province.

Simeon, Marie   Regina
b. April 7, 1905   Regina, Northwest Territories

Marie's stories illustrated a career born in a sketchbook. At the age of 17, Marie moved from Regina to Paris to study
fashion design. During her three years of study in Europe, her dress and hat designs were shown in New York, Minneapolis,
and Winnipeg. A family emergency brought her back to Regina where she put her newly acquired knowledge to work by
opening her own design studio. Marie's studio closed with her retirement in 1985.

Barrowman, Robert L.   Foam Lake
b. September 24, 1905   Scotland

"I'm proud to be a farmer," Bob informed me. "I've done it all my life." Born in Scotland, Bob moved with his family to a farm in the
Foam Lake area in 1911. Eventually, he ran his own mixed farm. While farming was full-time work, Bob always managed to set aside
some time to pursue his other interests, particularly baseball, curling, and dancing. Although Bob officially retired from farming in
1999, he continues to own his land.

Siggelkow, Mary   Coronach
b. March 2, 1905   Forget, Northwest Territories

An active and athletic young woman, Mary was crowned "Beauty Queen" at the age of 16. She enjoyed dancing and often attended the dances held in her community. A very capable cook, she ran her own restaurant. For Mary, getting married was remembered as the best time in her life.

Hancheruk, Nick   Foam Lake
b. December 9, 1904   Sheho, Northwest Territories

Nick and I talked about farming, its challenges, and the many changes that have had an impact on the business of farming over the years. He reminisced about his interest in raising and selling horses. Nick also remembered buying a car in 1927 and never receiving a ticket or a traffic fine of any kind in his entire life. "I was a good driver," he explained. When asked what advice he could offer others, he replied, "Take life easy."

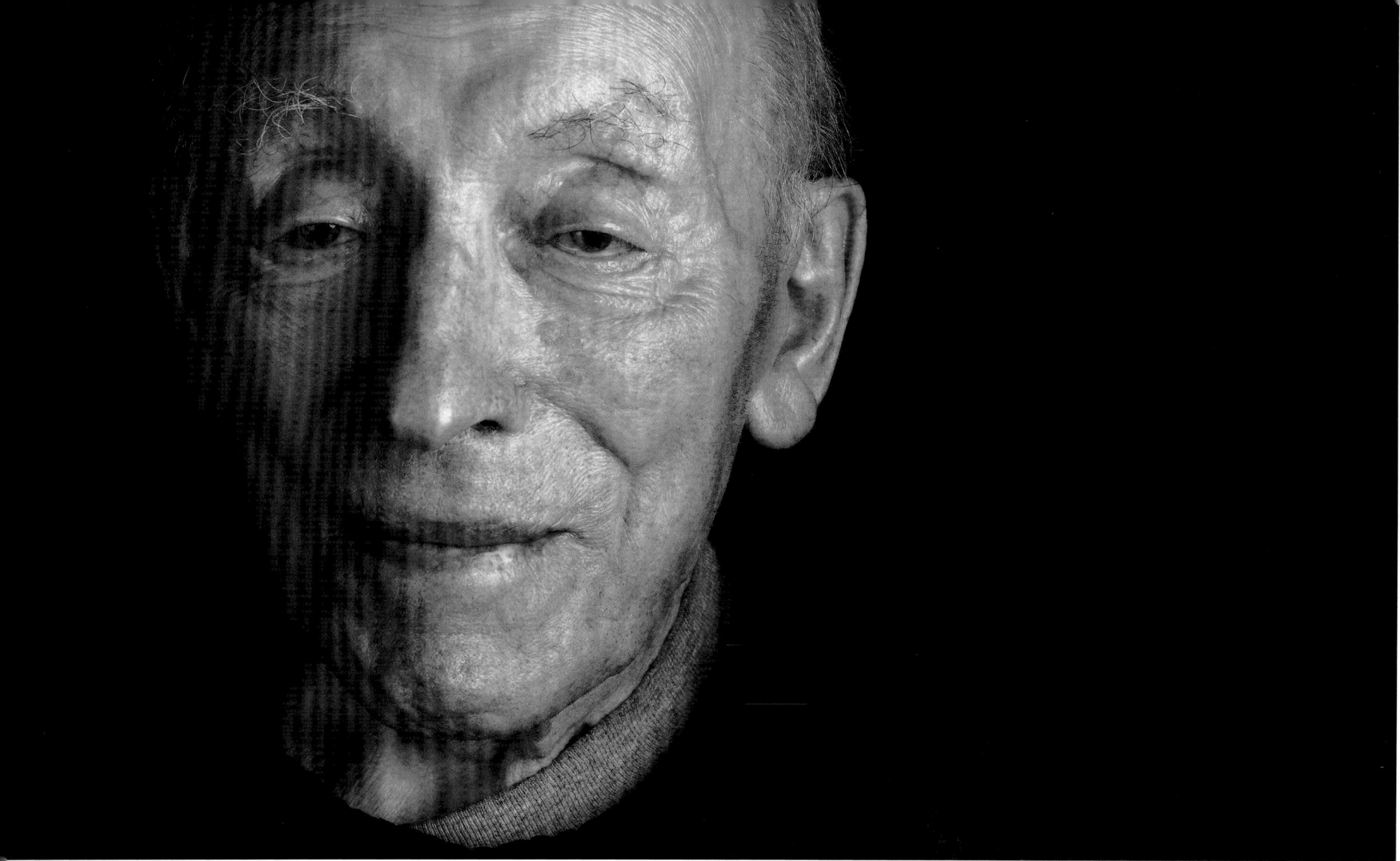

Brodner, Gregory   Muenster
b. April 6, 1905   Regina, Northwest Territories

The sixth of fifteen children, Gregory grew up on the family homestead south of Dysart. He became a Brother in the Benedictine Order at St. Peter's Abbey after two of his brothers had studied there. Farm work appealed to Gregory and for several years he used his talents at the Abbey's farm. In later years, Gregory maintained the Abbey's water system and kept the generator and furnace in good repair. He enjoyed fishing and reported once catching a 12 pound jackfish.

Kirtzinger, Clementine   Cudworth
b. October 11, 1904   Leofnard, Northwest Territories

Clementine's family moved to Canada in 1903 and immediately constructed a sod house on their homestead. It was into this home that Clementine was born a year later. Eventually, her father used logs to build a house, stables, and blacksmith shop. Clementine married in 1927 and she and her husband set up their farm near Bremen. Eight children soon followed. Gardening held a special interest for Clementine and she recalled working in the garden between 5:30 and 6:00 a.m. because it was the coolest part of the day. Later in life, Clementine pursued her interest in art and began painting.

Kaleka, Frances   Saskatoon
b. August 22, 1899   Northwest Territories

Frances welcomed me into her home and introduced me to the important people and events in her life by showing me the photographs of her family members displayed on her walls. At 106 years of age, this amazing, independent woman continues to live in her own home. Still interested in the events of her community and the world, she reads the newspaper everyday.

Flaten, Svea   Weyburn
b. August 5, 1905   Dalesburg, South Dakota

Svea got married in 1925. It was the very first wedding she ever attended. Following the wedding, Svea and her husband moved to the farm and began to fill their home with five children. Farm life suited Svea just fine. She was devoted to working on the farm and tending the garden. When asked to describe the best time of her life, Svea happily answered, "It's all been good!"

Campbell, Lillian V.   Tisdale
b. March 18, 1904   Niche, North Dakota

Through my conversation with Lillian, it became obvious that her caring nature was a strong thread that pulled through her life. She met her future husband when she was called upon to care for his arm. A good cook, she fed and cared for their three children. When asked what she believed contributed to her longevity, she answered, "I eat well and I take care of myself."

Gorst, Jean Meadow Lake
b. October 30, 1905 Eastham, England

Jean and her mother moved to the Meadow Lake area to assist her brother in establishing a homestead. Farm life did not appeal to Jean's mother and she returned to England. However, Jean remained and by 1927, she had married and was helping her husband set up a farm in the Briarsdale district. Eventually, the couple moved to Meadow Lake so their children could attend school. Jean became very active in her community. A member of the hospital auxiliary and her church choir, she also worked as the town's librarian for 27 years. Still active, Jean continues to enjoy exercising, walking, and reading.

Dashwood, Nellie   Maryfield
b. May 1, 1903   Hampstead, England

Like many immigrants, Nellie travelled to Canada by ship. Her journey was made memorable because the ship on which she was sailing made its crossing in May 1912, just one month after the sinking of the Titanic. During the journey across the Atlantic Ocean, Nellie's ship stopped briefly in the area where the Titanic had been lost. Arriving in Canada, Nellie's father found work as a blacksmith and the family grew up in town. An educated woman, Nellie taught in small country schools and worked for a time for the newspaper in Yorkton.

Letwenuk, Elizabeth   Foam Lake
b. March 14, 1904   Buchanan, Northwest Territories

When her mother began working in the fields of their farm, the housekeeping duties fell to ten year old Elizabeth. She learned to bake bread in a traditional Ukrainian outdoor clay oven, a method of baking she continued to use on her own farm after she married in 1918. Never idle, Elizabeth tended a garden one acre in size, often producing two barrels of sauerkraut from the cabbages grown. She raised sheep and spun the wool on her own spinning wheel. Old clothes were given new life as quilts. In the midst of all this activity, she still managed to find time to provide help to others and to entertain her friends.

Sanderson, Inez   Moose Jaw
b. September 7, 1905   Peoria, Illinois

A land grant convinced Inez's family to relocate to Saskatchewan from Illinois. Establishing a farm required a great deal of work by all members of the family. For Inez, this meant there was little time for schooling. She met her future husband at a local dance, recalling that he was tall and handsome and played in the band. Inez identified married life with her young children as the best time of her life. "My husband," she added, "was great with the children."

Sanford, Hazel   Saskatoon
b. November 6, 1905   Virden, Manitoba

Hazel and her family moved to Saskatchewan from Manitoba when she was four years old. As a young adult, she worked in a
hospital. She married in 1928 and raised two children. Her husband died in 1988 after 60 years of marriage. Throughout her life,
Hazel enjoyed reading and dancing, two activities that seemed appropriate given her advice to me. "Keep your mind and body active."

Kleiter, Leo   Saskatoon
b. August 25, 1903   Wisconsin

Leo acknowledged that his fondest memories centered on married life. Married in 1929, Leo and his wife raised three
children on the family farm near Cudworth. While I took his photograph, Leo described for me the box camera he used as
a young adult. He recalled enjoying the opportunity it provided him to develop the negatives himself and create his own
prints.

McColl, Emma M.   Estevan
b. August 15, 1903   Winnipeg, Manitoba

Emma and her husband lived in Estevan where he was a minister in the Apostolic Church. It was here that she began a long career as a piano teacher. Many of her talented students were recognized through the Royal Conservatory of Music and received awards at local music festivals and provincial competitions.

Humphrey, Ella   St. Walburg
b. January 10, 1903   South Dakota

"The best time in my life was when I was young," Ella told me. It was a time filled with socializing, music and lots of dancing. Shortly after her marriage in 1926, Ella and her husband began setting up their own farm. Interested in the fur industry, their farming operation included the raising and selling of minks. Skilled in fine handwork, Ella taught sewing and enjoyed tatting. She also actively participated in curling and square dancing.

Giesbrecht, Anna   Warman
b. August 14, 1904   Osler, Northwest Territories

Anna's family moved to Canada from Russia in the 1870's. Eventually they purchased a homestead near Osler and Anna was born.
Anna married and raised six sons on the original family homestead. Handed down over several generations, the farm is still
operated by members of her family. Anna loved to garden and continues to take pleasure in visiting the gardens in her community.

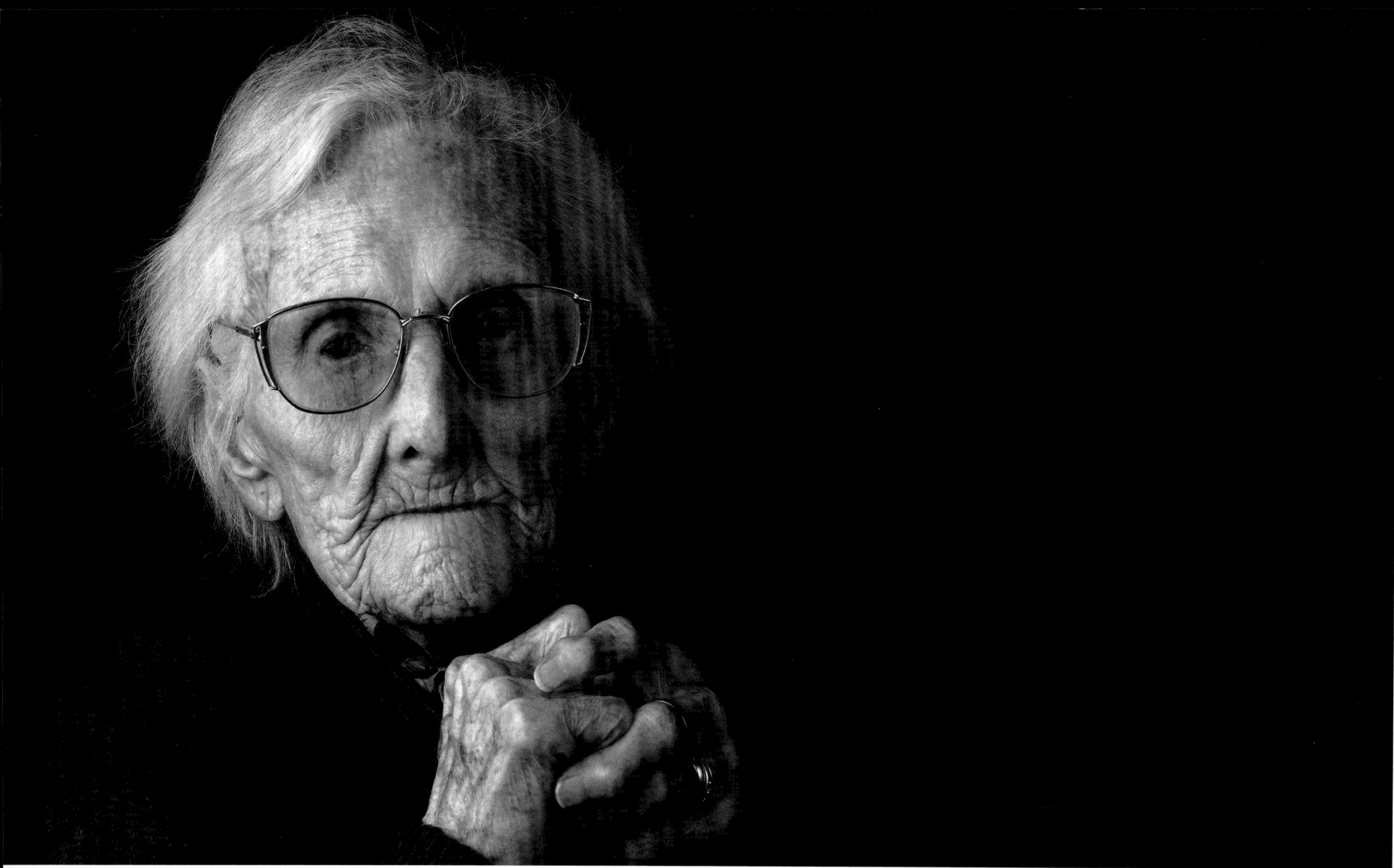

Ostlund, Elsa   Choiceland
b. November 21, 1905   Thief River Falls, Minnesota

Elsa grew up on the family farm in the Willow Glen area of the province, across the road from her grandparent's farm.
Elsa's family raised both cattle and sheep and sold cream in nearby Wadena. Everyone helped on the farm and one of Elsa's
duties was to ride her horse out to the fields every evening and bring the cattle home. Elsa was married in 1924 and, with
her husband, spent periods of time operating a farm, running a cafe, and picking berries. Eventually, they set up a farm at
Choiceland, a community where Elsa continues to live.

Chartier, Ethel I. North Battleford
b. January 10, 1903 Morrisburg, Ontario

Ethel moved from Regina to Turtle Lake in northern Saskatchewan where her husband worked as a barber and as a lay minister for the Apostolic Church. While there, Ethel operated a small ice cream parlour for a brief period of time. A good cook and able host, Ethel's kitchen was always ready to spring into action. This proved fortunate, as her husband would often bring people home for dinner.

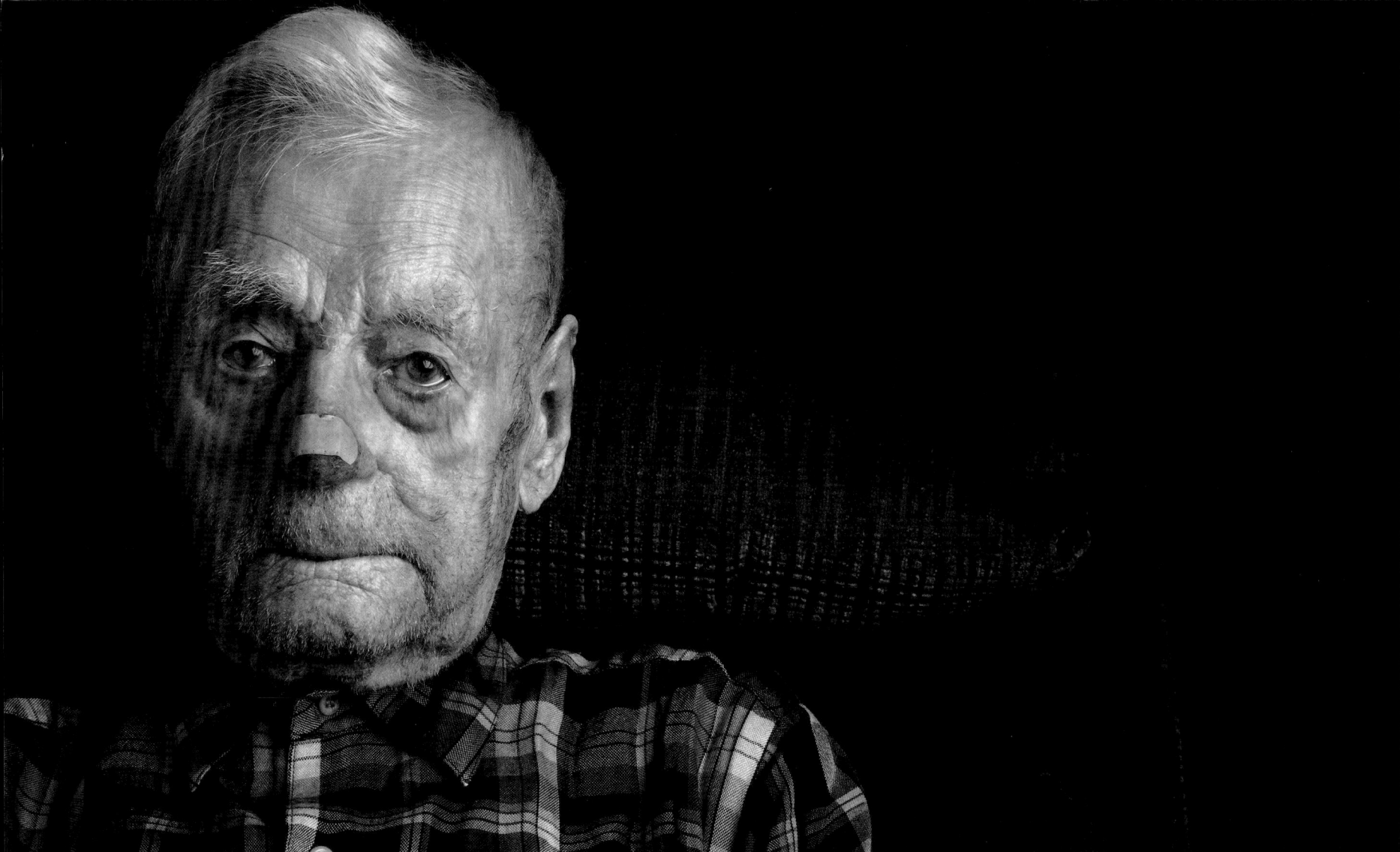

Bargen, Gerhard J.   Saskatoon
b. March 1, 1903   Schoenau No. 13, Sagradovka, Ukraine

The dreadful conditions resulting from the Bolshevik Revolution were the driving force behind Gerhard's decision to move his family to Canada. Settling first near Blumenhoff , the family eventually purchased land in the Glenbush area. Arriving at their new homestead and finding it no longer available, the family had to spend the winter in a neighbour's newly constructed chicken coop. Happily, the following spring, Gerhard obtained a quarter section of land and the family set about establishing a farm.

Machin, Dorothy Louise   Regina
b. May 4, 1905   Illinois

A teacher by profession, Dorothy had a number of interests outside of her career. She loved to dance and play the piano. "I took a lot of music lessons," she admitted. She also sewed her own clothing. While Dorothy was fond of a variety of card games, Bridge was really her game, having belonged to two Bridge clubs over the years. She also loved to entertain and continued to plan parties and functions for family and friends until she was in her 90's.

Roberts, Kathleen   Prince Albert
b. March 01, 1903   London, England

Listening to Kit talk about her life, one fact quickly became evident. She has always been a woman in motion. Along with participating on a woman's softball team, she found the time and energy to tend a large garden, raise three children, and play the organ at her church. Her list of public recognitions includes the title of "Best Chicken Plucker". Entering a walk-a-thon at age 64, Kit successfully completed the trek from Prince Albert to Shellbrook. She learned to drive a car at the age of 74.

Pederson, Lucy E.   Coronach
b. November 6, 1899   Parham, Ontario

Many of Lucy's fondest memories were of her childhood. She remembered her mother as a wonderful cook who could "make a meal out of nothing." A quiet man, her father liked to walk several miles everyday. Lucy played the piano and organ, often performing in her brothers' band. As a young mother, Lucy helped out in the fields during harvest time. She would collect the sheaves as they came out of the binder and stook them on the ground. If she had a small baby with her, she would put the baby in a wooden box and carry the baby from stook to stook.

Block, Samuel   Saskatoon
b. September 10, 1904   Russia

Samuel had such a wonderful sense of humour that many of his stories seemed to be strung together with his laughter. He reminisced about the time he was farming with eight horses. When he lost one of the horses in a well, he decided it might be a good time to consider buying a tractor. He shared stories about buying two sections of land for nineteen thousand dollars, about installing lights on his new tractor so he could work later into the evening, about a conversation he was once had with Tommy Douglas, and about his children. A devout man, Samuel continues to read the Bible everyday.

MacIssac, Elizabeth Mary   Saskatoon
b. December 27, 1893   New Brunswick

Mary was an inspiration. At 112 years of age, she answered my questions with a touch of humour and laughter. The mother of five, Mary raised her children in Prince Albert where her husband practiced law. She took pleasure in playing the piano for her family in the evenings. On the day of my visit, she recited poetry and played the piano for me.

Bexson, Harry Allan Frenchman Butte
b. January 10, 1904 Derby, England

Harry is a man who has lived his life to the fullest. Moving to Saskatchewan from England in 1921, his love of horses led him to a lifelong interest in the rodeo. He participated as a bronco rider and continues to attend rodeos on a regular basis. Harry and his wife raised nine children on their ranch near Meadow Lake. When I asked him his secret to a long life, he replied, "I don't have one. I smoked, drank, and have eaten everything I wanted and I'm still here. You tell me."

Lamson, Bessie K.   Yorkton
b. January 3, 1898   Deloraine, Manitoba

Bessie moved with her family to Yorkton in the autumn of 1902. One year later, the family relocated to a farm at Rokeby. Bessie spent her childhood on that farm and years later, after she married Ernest Lamson, she and her husband continued to farm in the Rokeby area. Bessie and her husband retired from farming after 66 years.

Goertzen, Helena Rosthern
b. January 24, 1905   United States of America

Helena remembered her mother as a wonderful cook who always made sure vegetables were included in the meals. She credited her early exposure to vegetables for her longevity. A recipe known as "potato noodles" was one of her family's favourite dishes. Throughout her life, Helena attended local dances on a regular basis. Her favourite dances were old-time waltzes and the two-step.

Doerksen, Abraham   Rosthern
b. February 15, 1898   Manitoba

Soft-spoken, Abraham recollected getting married in 1924 and raising two children on the family's farm. His eyes lit up and he smiled at the memory of the joy he and wife found in dancing.

Zacher, Mearl   Yorkton
b. October 29, 1903   Glosston, North Dakota

Mearl loved participating in family activities, especially picnics, wiener roasts, and Sunday rides in the car. She had an interest in cooking and was well-known for her saskatoon berry pies, dill pickles, and deep fried battered wieners. Mearle loved to square dance and, along with her husband, was active in the Bows and Bells dance club. Gardening was another area that gave her pleasure. She would often deliver flowers from her garden to family members and friends as a way to brighten their days.

Brooks, Isola   Saskatoon
b. October 19, 1904   Cash County, Iowa

Born in Iowa, Isola homesteaded with her family near Arcola. As a young adult, she worked as a telephone operator. Her interests over the years have included reading, crocheting, playing the piano, and dancing. A lover of the outdoors, Isola always enjoyed opportunities to go for a drive in the country.

Goud, Mildred   Estevan
b. October 17, 1905   Kingston, Ontario

Mildred's family farmed north of Estevan. Following her marriage to her school sweetheart, Mildred and her husband established their own farm where they lived and worked for 65 years. During that time, Mildred was active in a variety of community projects and events, often taking on leadership roles. She and her husband retired to Estevan in 1988.

Switzer, Evelyn   Regina
b. November 2, 1900   Yorkton, Northwest Territories

In the course of our conversation, Evelyn revealed to me that longevity is a tradition in her family. Her mother lived to the age of 99 and her brother lived to 106 years of age. A graduate of the University of Saskatchewan, Evelyn taught Kindergarten and Grade One in Regina schools for 40 years. Near the end of her teaching career, her students took to calling her "Granny". For Evelyn, it was a term of endearment. "I always thought it was so cute."

Hladun, Sadie   Canora
b. August 31, 1905   Gorlitz, Northwest Territories

Raising her three sons on the family farm, Sadie lived the traditional farm life. Her garden was large and well-tended and she was a very good cook. A firm believer in maintaining a connection with one's culture, Sadie worked hard to keep the traditions of her Ukrainian heritage strong. She, her husband and children spoke the Ukrainian language at home. A progressive woman, she taught her sons to repair their own clothes.

Bancroft, Eileen M.   Regina
b. May 24, 1904   Arcola, Northwest Territories

A cheerful woman, Eileen chatted easily about her memories of growing up in southern Saskatchewan. She recalled her father, the superintendent of the Western Grain Association, moving the family to Regina from Arcola in 1913. Sometime shortly after the move, Eileen contracted typhoid fever and had to be hospitalized. Her fondest memories are from her recent past. "The best time in my life," Eileen beamed, "was when my nephew, George Michael Bancroft, received the Order of Canada."

Miller, Gladys Mildred   Foam Lake
b. April 21, 1904   England

Gladys shared with me stories of taking the train to school when she lived in England and of travelling by train from Halifax to Saskatchewan when the family moved to Canada.   Gladys recalled sewing and tennis as activities she enjoyed. When asked to identify the best time in her life, she did not hesitate. "Now is the best time!" she replied.

Eberhardt, Emma   Lang
b. April 19, 1904   Lang, Northwest Territories

Emma greeted me with a smile at the door of the house in which she has lived since 1944. Leading me into her living room, she sat in her favourite chair and shared the stories of her life with me. Growing up on the farm, the middle of nine children, she remembered her mother tending a huge garden and raising geese. She met her future husband when he came from Winnipeg to help with the harvest at the neighbouring farm. They married when she was 16, moved into town, and raised four children.

Johnson, Clara   Redvers
b. March 23, 1898   London, England

Educated in Moose Jaw, Clara attended normal school in Regina before embarking on a teaching career. She taught in several schools in the province and eventually took a teaching assignment at Lightning Creek, south of Redvers. It was here that Clara met her future husband. Following their marriage in 1922, Clara and her husband moved to a farm near the hamlet of Frys and settled into their lives as farmers. It was a career that would span more than 45 years.

Scott, Evelyn   Humboldt
b. September 20, 1904   England

Feisty and energetic, Evelyn shared stories of coming to Canada as a six year old orphan and of living with foster parents until reaching the age of 25. She and her husband operated a mixed farm and while running the farm was often hard work, Evelyn was thrilled with the opportunity it gave her to care for animals. She is a woman of varied interests. A self-taught artist working primarily with watercolour and pastels, Evelyn has completed 20 to 30 pieces of art. She continues to be an avid fan of professional wrestler Stone Cold Austin.

McIntosh, Rosalie   Watrous
b. May 24, 1902   Glenella, Manitoba

Rosalie's father, and later her mother, ran general stores in Yorkton and in the small community of Otthon. With the death of both of her parents, Rosalie moved to Melville where met and married Jack McIntosh. Rosalie was an active member of her church. A talented seamstress and avid gardener, she often took on the task of sewing vestments for the local priests and of providing floral arrangements for the church altar. Her petit point and needlepoint pictures are the prized possessions of friends and family.

Sabourin, Justine Prince Albert
b. January 30, 1904   Batoche Area, Northwest Territories

A sweet lady, visiting with Justine was truly a pleasure. Greeting me with a smile, she happily shared the stories of her life: being raised by her grandmother, cooking for the Department of Natural Resources at a bush camp, and working in her garden. Still interested in following events as they unfold in her community and around the world, Justine reads the newspaper everyday and continues to socialize every Saturday night over games of cribbage.

185

Hrechuk, Dmytro   Saskatoon
b. November 5, 1905   Sambor, Ukraine

Over a glass of wine, Dmytro reminisced about the many paths he has followed in his life. Born in Ukraine, he arrived in
Canada in time for the start of the Great Depression. During the decade of uncertainty that followed, he worked whenever
and wherever jobs were available. When there were no jobs to be had, he packed his bags and lived the life of a hobo.
Eventually life improved. Dmytro and his wife travelled to Saskatchewan on a holiday and, feeling at home in the province,
bought a farm which Dmytro ran until he retired.

Snow, Zella W.   Saskatoon
b. June 1, 1905   Collingwood, Ontario

Zella came to Saskatchewan in 1910 and grew up in the community of Caron. Following her graduation from Grade 12, Zella became a teacher and taught in small rural schools. She recalled that the life of a teacher in those days was an interesting experience. Zella often lived in the school. From time to time, farmers would drop by to deliver food. At the end of every month, Zella would be paid $10.00 and given a promissory note. She left the profession when she married. Her advice to others is simple: "Live life day-to-day."

Letkemann, Jacob H.   Rosthern
b. January 17, 1905   Chortitz, Russia

Sharp and witty, Jacob filled our conversation with laughter. Born into a family of 21 in Russia, Jacob moved to Saskatchewan in 1923 to work on a farm. It proved to be a wise move for Jacob. Not only was working on the farm a good experience, he ended up marrying the boss's daughter. When asked about the best time in his life, he remarked that his wedding day was "the best day I ever had!" It was a union that lasted nearly 70 years.

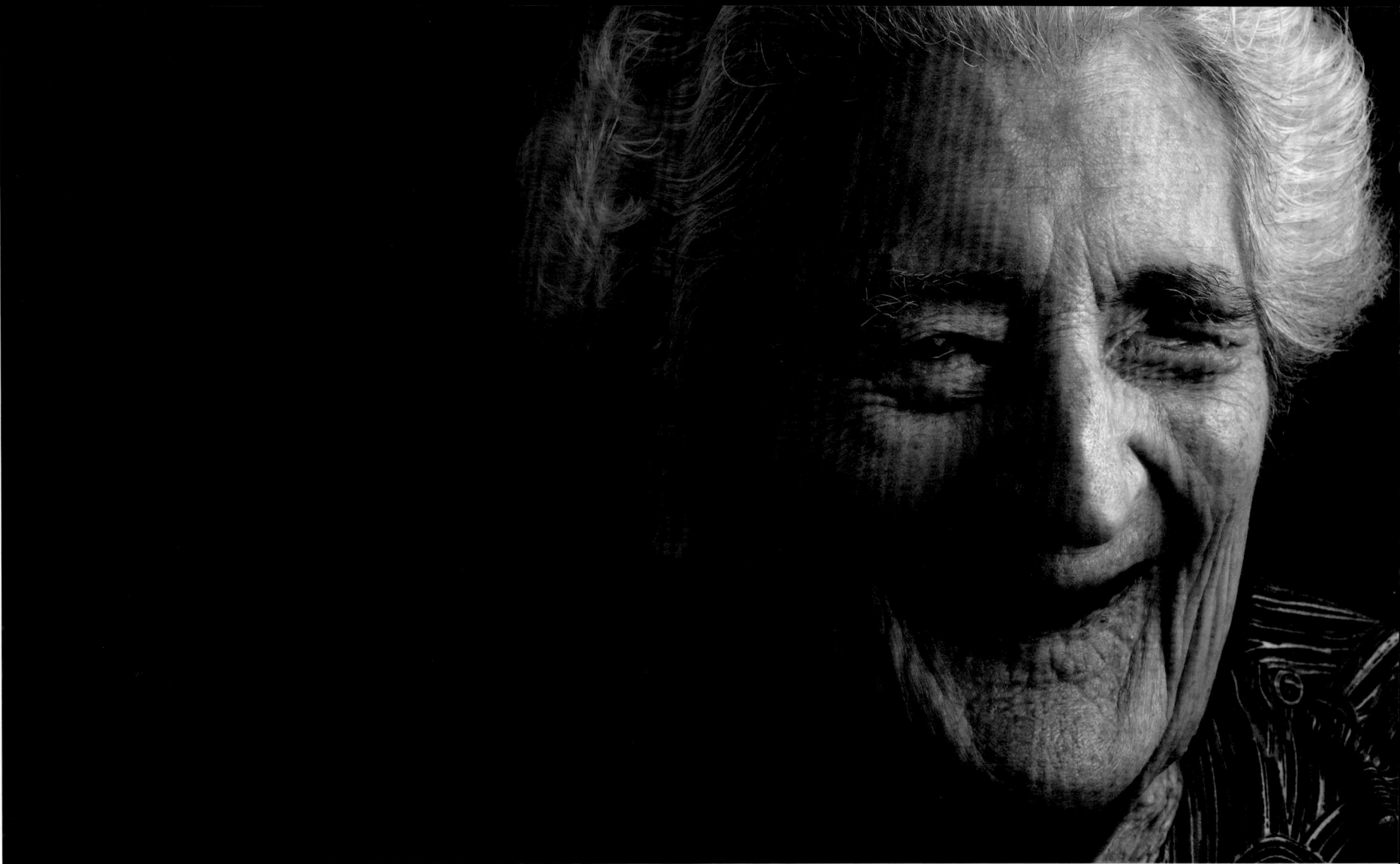

Rondeau, Leonne E.   Regina
b. October 8, 1902   Rawdon, Quebec

Leonne and her husband moved to Rouleau in 1920. There she raised their two children and assisted her husband in his dental practice. A lifelong gardener, Leonne also enjoyed playing cribbage and Bridge. According to her family, Leonne has always been a happy, positive person who loves life.

Millar, A. Pearl   North Battleford
b. September 18, 1903   Moose Jaw, Northwest Territories

As an only child growing up on the farm near Tuxford, Pearl had the opportunity to participate in all aspects of farming. Although she was trained for careers as a secretary and a teacher, it was farming that guided her life. When her father died, Pearl and her husband returned to operate the family farm. Her early introduction to farming gave her the knowledge and confidence she needed to successfully run the farm. As Pearl noted, there were many times she would stay in the fields all day so she could tell the hired man what to do.

Cottingham, Bessie   Swift Current
b. February 19, 1903   Ontario

Bessie had very little hearing and poor eyesight, but she was gracious and dignified and sat proudly for her portrait. Having been an avid reader over the course of her life, Bessie still maintained a love of language. During our visit she recited the following poem for me; "Lightning flashed and thunder rolled, the Earth was all a shakin'. The pig curled up his tail and ran to save his bacon."

Jansen, Appolonia   Macklin
b. February, 4, 1904   Minnesota

Lonie is no stranger to large families. The eldest of 15 children, Lonie married when she was 18 years of age. She and her husband set up their own farm and it became home to their 14 children. Life on the farm was filled with activity. She always kept a large garden and spent a good deal of time in the kitchen. She never learned to drive. "I was too busy with the kids," she admitted.

Mundt, Caroline   Yorkton
b. June 1, 1903   Tulcea, Romania

Caroline moved to Canada in 1914. Her father was a shoemaker and Caroline remembered having to work as a young girl in order to help the family survive. When she married at the age of 16, she and her husband moved to a farm in the McNutt area of the province. Farm life was hard work. She often helped in the fields, forming the sheaves of wheat into stooks.   Caroline loved baking and visiting with friends over a cup of tea and a plate of cookies.

Herman, Mary   Guernsey
b. December 4, 1904   Manitoba

Mary's children spoke to me about her love of gardening, card playing, and crocheting. Having only flown on an airplane
once in her lifetime, Mary's usual method of transportation was to travel by train. According to her family, Mary believes
she has lived a long life because she is honest, stubborn, and genuinely interested in people.

Olekson, Katharine   Saskatoon
b. July 30, 1904   Ukraine

Katharine's husband was a carpenter in Ukraine and she moved to Canada with him in 1924. A capable and willing worker, Katharine sustained a large garden on their property. She took pleasure in nurturing her garden all season and sharing its bounty with others in the fall. Her other interests included baking, playing cards, and doing embroidery. An Orthodox Ukrainian, Katharine attended church every week.

MARK GRESCHNER

Mark Greschner is a Master Photographer. His work has received many national and international awards.

Born and raised in Saskatchewan, Mark has never felt a need to live elsewhere. He currently resides in Regina with his wife and two children.

INDEX